A BALLAD FOR KITTY COCKROACH

Words and Pictures
by
Keith Chandler

Fair Acre Press

Miss Pretty Kitty Cockroach
come sit upon my knee
(or one of them). I will tell the story
of How Things Used To Be.

The sky was dark, bin liner black.
For seven years and a day
the planet shuddered in its track.
The blood froze in our veins, they say.

For seven years nothing flew nor grew.
No song was heard, no sound
except the sighing of the wind
around the dying land.

No day, no night, no dark, no light.
No sun, no moon were seen.
No spring, no fall, no differences at all.
No blue. No pink. No green.

Deep in the fissures of the rock
we trembled head to head.
Brown warriors in a field of shields
we scarcely breathed, played dead

for seven years, for seven long years,
our spiracles gone numb.
That was until the Great White Roach
proclaimed our time had come.

Lights in the sky were dimly seen.
Blood red the darkness thinned.
Then one by one from crack and stone
we crept into our Promised Land.

You may read it in The Prophets –
before that seven years' night
the Earth was ruled by upright fools
who drove us out of sight.

They built these towns like termite mounds
mile high where nothing stirs,
these ribbon roads of concrete
for petrol charioteers.

They soared like silver insects
but crashed as heaps of scrap,
their fuselages headless –
wing cases broken, thoraxes snapped.

They say before the spinning stopped
this Earth was full of grace –
a jewel uniquely beautiful
in the black velvet box of time and space.

The Earth was like a garden.
Colours hung from the sky
in glittering drops. Rivers ran
where ruminants watched the hours roll by.

Plants flowered in graceful fountains.
Grass grew like a weed.
More food & fruit from branch & root
than any cockroach child might need.

Our planet teemed with creatures,
feathered, furred and finned
who crawled and ran and flew and swam –
a pan-harmonious hymn.

The seasons turned like Beauty.
The great green planet sang
to itself, a spinning top,
or like a beautiful glass goblet rang.

Now what is left? A desert
where nothing good remains
but glass and rags and plastic bags,
wind-blown paper, wind-picked bones.

Maybe it was because their brains
evolved behind their eyes
stopped Human Beings from clearly seeing
and made them so unwise?

Our brains are scattered from our snouts
along our proto-spines
and down our legs – each one of us
a multiplicity of minds.

They thought they were so clever,
found pools of fossil sun –
power to shake the night awake,
a million trillion lights switched on .

But they were greedy, needed stuff
to dress themselves, to stuff
themselves, or stuff with other stuff
and stuff like that. They never had enough.

They lived for Self Indulgence
and Novelty – had toys
to make a child grow wide-eyed wild,
especially those cockroach boys.

With brisk aplomb they made a bomb
brighter than the poor old sun,
invented steeds like centipedes
faster than a hundred legs can run.

Had living pictures on their walls
and in their hands had *phones*
to talk without antennae stalk –
invisibly, no pheromones.

And when they tired of doing that
had *holidays* and *sport.*
And when they tired of doing that
they fought.

They took our garden paradise
and turned it to a dump,
the good earth soiled with gas and oil –
their civilisation's sump.

The Everliving Cockroach –
Eternal Praises be upon His Name –
tells how, when The Great Darkness fell,
they only had themselves to blame.

They picked on us, The Chosen Ones,
and drove us underground
beneath the floors to feed perforce
on what they left behind.

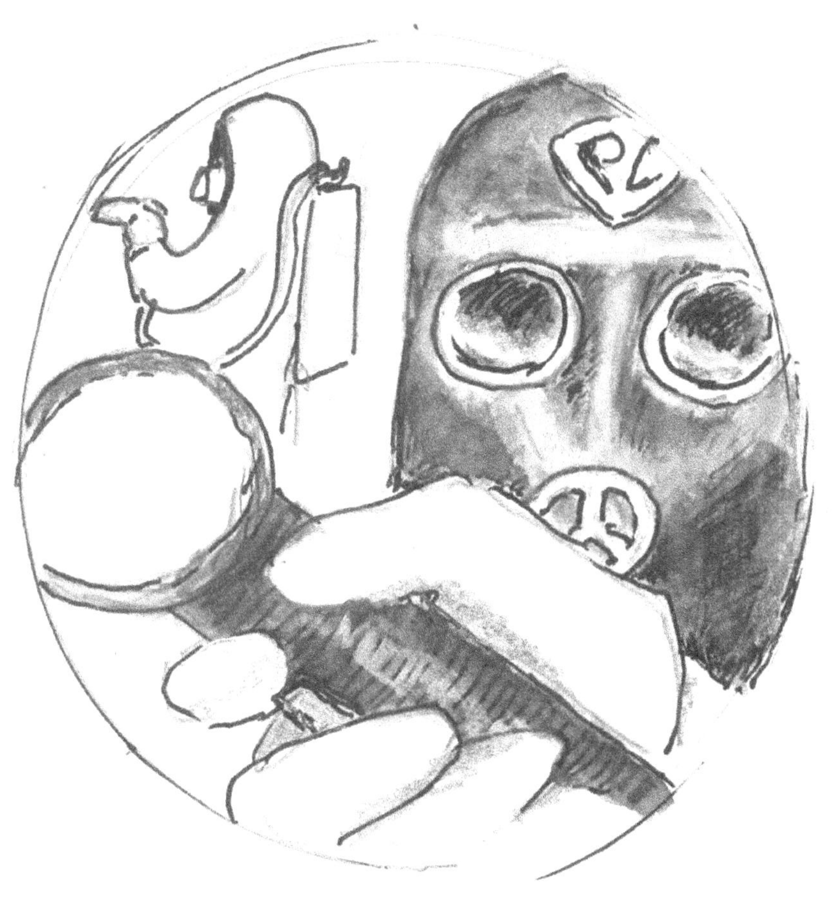

They hunted us with chemicals
strapped to their backs. For fun
they hunted us. Their battle cry
"Look I have squished another one!"

Such fear they bore our forebears –
but not to be compared
to their hatred for each other
for what they could have shared.

We heard the sounds of fighting,
the radiant blast of bombs
that turned their homes to catacombs,
not once but countless times.

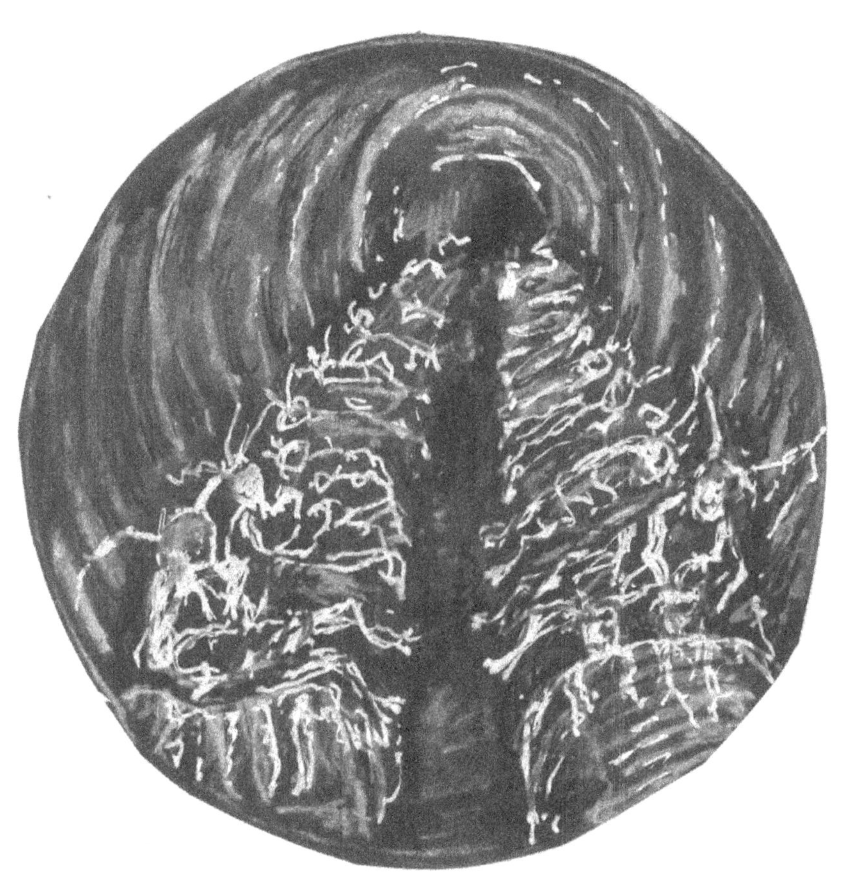

Deep in our shelters underground
we trembled, held our breath.
We waved our feelers for the scent
of life. What we smelt was DEATH.

Miss Pretty Kitty Cockroach
my compound eyes are filled with tears
when I recall the horror
of those pre-Cockroach years.

Though I am old and white-tipped,
not many layers left to shed,
I lift my arms in supplication
mantis-like above my head

and pray to The Great Cockroach
who dwells beyond distress
to keep us free from apathy
excreting such a mess.

"Can we begin to make amends?"
your odours seem to ask.
O my dear grub, my whiskered friend,
that is our solemn task.

We cockroaches are blest, we make
the best of what we find.
We forage, share together, speak
with pheromones of one mind.

Together we may cleanse the crust
of stuff that like a curse
they left behind – we sweep the air,
our sensitive long feelers going first.

We tend the poisoned furrows.
We study hard to learn
from our best cockroach scientists
to make the Garden Time return.

Little Miss Kitty Cockroach
hissing so prettily
through mandibles and sideways teeth
now you must promise me

growing from nymph to adult
that you will try to care
for this poor ruined planet –
and never take more than your share.

Bless and forgive all forms of life.
Even the Human Race
so much more loathsome than ourselves
I daresay has its place.

 Fair Acre Press

First published in Great Britain in 2019
by Fair Acre Press

www.fairacrepress.co.uk

Copyright © Keith Chandler 2019

A CIP catalogue record of this book is available from
the British Library.

ISBN 978-1-911048-39-8

About Keith Chandler

Born in Nigeria, educated at Christs Hospital and
New College, Oxford, Keith Chandler worked as a
schoolteacher in Liverpool, London and Norfolk.

His latest collection, *The Goldsmiths Apprentice,* was
awarded *The International Rubery Award*
for best independently published poetry collection
in 2018, the title poem also winning
a runner-up prize in the National Poetry competition.

Previous publications

Ten English Poets (Carcanet 1977)

Kett's Rebellion (Carcanet 1982)

A Passing Trade (O.H.P. 1992)

A Different Kind of Smoke (Redbeck 2000)

The English Civil War Part 2 (Peterloo Poets 2008)

The Grandpa Years (Fair Acre Press 2014)

The Goldsnith's Apprentice (Fair Acre Press 2018)

Some Responses to *The English Civil War Part 2*

And now, with a fanfare, comes the Court Jester, Keith Chandler, though as good jesters do he speaks unwelcome truths. Read this hilarious and mordant book.
Peter Scupham, Poetry Review

A spellbinding book – tremendously impressive, entertaining, moving, funny. And original. These poems are always 'about' something.
Anthony Thwaite

His angle on the world is often fresh and funny, equipped with formidable confidence in the face of uncomfortable truths.
Rennie Parker, Critical Survey

It is a humane, funny, sometimes biting, very English collection, with a strong apocalyptic theme running through ... A genuine poet, remarkable for his acuteness of observation and unshowy craftsmanship.
George Szirtes, Poetry Review

Some Responses to *The Goldsmith's Apprentice*

This is a fresh, nuanced and humane collection of poems
with its eye and ear to the world of work in particular,
and to the craft of survival in general.

It is a wonderful and generous book.

The poems welcome you in and hold your attention
with their deftness, attentiveness and joy in making.
David Morley
Winner of The Ted Hughes Award

Crammed with good ideas and strong endings,
these are accessible poems which are deeply engaged
with both the ephemera and the big issues
of ordinary lives.

More than anything, I value them
for their great humanity.

To appropriate the ending of a wonderfully moving poem
about a nurse, these poems, coming as they do
out of the best motivations and the deepest artistic rigour,
are The Real Thing.
Jonathan Edwards
Winner of The Costa Award for Poetry

www.ingramcontent.com/pod-product-compliance
Lightning Source LLC
Chambersburg PA
CBHW050021040726
47599CB00014B/1488